Rubaíyat
of
Omar Khayyam

ISBN: 1 84013 378 3

Copyright © Axiom Publishing 2001

This edition produced for Grange Books
Units 1-6 Kingsnorth Ind. Est.
Hoo, Nr. Rochester
Kent ME3 9ND
United Kingdom
www.grangebooks.co.uk

Grange Books PLC

Rubaiyat of Omar Khayyam

Illustrations by
Andrew Peno

Grange
BOOKS

I

Awake! for Morning in the
Bowl of Night
Has flung the Stone that puts
the Stars to Flight:
And Lo! the Hunter of the
East has caught
The Sultán's Turret in a
Noose of Light.

II

Dreaming when Dawn's Left
Hand was in the Sky
I heard a Voice within the
Tavern cry,
'Awake, my little ones, and
fill the Cup
Before Life's Liquor in its Cup
be dry.'

III

And, as the Cock crew, those
who stood before
The Tavern shouted — 'Open
then the Door!
You know how little while we
have to stay,
And, once departed, may
return no more.'

IV

Now the New Year reviving old
Desires,
The thoughtful Soul to
Solitude retires,
Where the White Hand of
Moses on the Bough
Puts out, and Jesus from the
Ground suspires.

V

Irám indeed is gone with all
its Rose,
And Jamshyd's Sev'n-ring'd
Cup where no one knows;
But still the Vine her ancient
Ruby yields,
And still a Garden by the
Water blows.

VI

And David's Lips are lock't;
but in divine
High piping Pehleví, with
'Wine! Wine! Wine!
Red Wine! —the Nightingale
cries to the Rose
That yellow cheek of hers to
incarnadine.

VII

Come, fill the Cup, and in the
Fire of Spring
The Winter Garment of
Repentance fling:
The Bird of Time has but a
little way To fly—and Lo!
the Bird is on the Wing.

VIII

And look—a thousand
Blossoms with the Day
Woke—and a thousand
scatter'd into Clay:
And this first Summer
Month that brings the Rose
Shall take Jamshyd and
Kaikobád away.

IX

But come with old Khayyám,
and leave the Lot
Of Kaikobád and Kaikhosrú
forgot:
Let Rustum lay about him as
he will,
Or Hátim Tai cry Supper—
heed them not.

X

With me along some Strip of
Herbage strown
That just divides the desert
from the sown,
Where name of Slave and
Sultán scarce is known,
And pity Sultán Máhmúd
on his Throne.

XI

Here with a Loaf of Bread
beneath the Bough,
A Flask of Wine, a Book of
Verse—and Thou
Beside me singing in the
Wilderness—
And Wilderness is Paradise
enow.

XII

'How sweet is mortal
Sovranty!'—think some:
Others— 'How blest the
Paradise to come!'
Ah, take the Cash in hand
and waive the Rest;
Oh, the brave Music of a
distant Drum!

XIII

Look to the Rose that blows
about us—'Lo,
Laughing,' she says, 'into the
World I blow:
At once the silken Tassel of
my Purse
Tear, and its Treasure on the
Garden throw.'

XIV

The worldly Hope men set
their Hearts upon
Turns Ashes—or it prospers;
and anon,
Like Snow upon the Desert's
dusty Face
Lighting a little Hour or
two—is gone.

XV

And those who husbanded the
Golden Grain,
And those who flung it to the
Winds like Rain,
Alike to no such aureate
Earth are turn'd
As, buried once, Men want
dug up again.

XVI

Think, in this batter'd
Caravanserai
Whose Doorways are
alternate Night and Day,
How Sultán after Sultán with
his Pomp
Abode his Hour or two, and
went his way.

XVII

They say the Lion and the
Lizard keep
The Courts where Jamshyd
gloried and drank deep,
And Bahrám, that great
Hunter—the Wild Ass
Stamps o'er his Head, and he
lies fast asleep.

XVIII

I sometimes think that never
blows so red
The Rose as where some
buried Caesar bled;
That every Hyacinth the
Garden wears
Dropt in its Lap from some
once lovely Head.

XIX

And this delightful Herb
whose tender Green
Fledges the River's Lip on
which we lean—
Ah, lean upon it lightly! for
who knows
From what once lovely Lip it
springs unseen!

XX

Ah, my Belovéd, fill the Cup
that clears
To-day of past Regrets and
future Fears—
To-morrow?—Why,
To-morrow I may be
Myself with Yesterday's
Sev'n Thousand Years.

XXI

Lo! some we loved, the loveliest
and the best
That Time and Fate of all
their Vintage prest,
Have drunk their Cup a
Round or two before,
And one by one crept silently
to Rest.

XXII

And we, that now make
merry in the Room
They left, and Summer
dresses in new Bloom,
Ourselves must we beneath
the Couch of Earth
Descend, ourselves to make a
Couch—for whom?

XXIII

Ah, make the most of what we
    yet may spend,
Before we too into the Dust
        descend;
Dust into Dust, and under
        Dust, to lie,
Sans Wine, sans Song, sans
    Singer, and
            —sans End!

XXIV

Alike for those who for To-day
        prepare,
And those that after a
    Tomorrow stare,
A muezzin from the Tower of
    Darkness cries
'Fools! your Reward is neither
    Here nor There!'

XXV

Why, all the Saints and
Sages who discuss'd
Of the Two Worlds so
learnedly, are thrust
Like foolish Prophets forth;
their Words to Scorn
Are scatter'd, and their
Mouths are stopt with Dust.

XXVI

Oh, come with old Khayyám,
and leave the Wise
To talk; one thing is certain,
that Life flies;
One thing is certain, and the
Rest is Lies;
The Flower that once has
blown for ever dies.

XXVII

Myself when young did
eagerly frequent
Doctor and Saint, and heard
great Argument
About it and about: but
evermore
Came out by the same Door
as in I went.

XXVIII

With them the Seed of Wisdom
did I sow,
And with my own hand
labour'd it to grow:
And this was all the Harvest
that I reap'd—
'I came like water, and like
Wind I go.'

XXIX

Into this universe, and why
not knowing,
Nor whence, like water willy-
nilly flowing;
And out of it, as wind along
the waste,
I know not whither, willy-
nilly blowing.

XXX

What, without asking, hither
hurried whence?
And, without asking, whither
hurried hence!
Another and another cup to
drown
The Memory of this
Impertinence!

XXXI

Up from Earth's Centre
through the Seventh Gate
I rose, and on the Throne of
Saturn sate,
And many Knots unravel'd
by the Road;
But not the Knot of Human
Death and Fate.

XXXII

There was a Door to which I
found no Key:
There was a Veil past which I
could not see:
Some little Talk awhile of Me
and Thee
There seem'd—and then no
more of Thee and Me.

XXXIII

Then to the rolling Heav'n
itself I cried,
Asking, 'What Lamp had
Destiny to guide
Her little children
stumbling in the Dark?'
And— 'A blind
understanding!' Heav'n
replied.

XXXIV

Then to this earthen Bowl did
I adjourn
My Lip the secret Well of Life
to learn:
And Lip to Lip it murmur'd—
'While you live
Drink!— for once dead you
never shall return.'

XXXV

I think the Vessel, that with fugitive
Articulation answer'd, once did live,
And merry-make; and the cold Lip I kiss'd
How many Kisses might it take—and give!

XXXVI

For in the Market-place, one Dusk of Day,
I watch'd the Potter thumping his wet Clay:
And with its all obliterated Tongue
It murmur'd—'Gently, Brother, gently, pray!'

XXXVII

Ah, fill the Cup:—what boots it
to repeat
How Time is slipping
underneath our Feet:
Unborn To-morrow, and
dead Yesterday
Why fret about them if To-
day be sweet!

XXXVIII

One Moment in
Annihilation's Waste,
One Moment, of the Well of
Life to taste—
The Stars are setting and the
Caravan
Starts for the Dawn of
Nothing—Oh, make haste!

XXXIX

How long, how long, in
definite Pursuit
Of This and That endeavour
and dispute?
Better be merry with the
fruitful Grape
Than sadder after none, or
bitter, Fruit.

XL

You know, my Friends, how
long since in my House
For a new Marriage I did
make Carouse:
Divorced old barren Reason
from my Bed,
And took the Daughter of the
Vine to Spouse.

XLI

For 'Is' and 'Is-not' though
with Rule and Line
And 'Up-and-down' without,
I could define,
I yet in all I only cared to
know,
Was never deep in anything
but—Wine.

XLII

And lately, by the Tavern
Door agape,
Came stealing through the
Dusk an Angel Shape
Bearing a Vessel on his
Shoulder; and
He bid me taste of it; and
'twas—the Grape!

XLIII

The Grape that can with Logic
absolute
The To-and-Seventy jarring
Sects confute:
The subtle Alchemist that in
a Trice
Life's leaden Metal into Gold
transmute

XLIV

The mighty Mahmúd, the
victorious Lord,
That all the misbelieving and
black Horde
Of Fears and Sorrows that
infest the Soul
Scatters and slays with his
enchanted Sword.

XLV

But leave the Wise to wrangle,
and with me
The Quarrel of the Universe
let be:
And, in some corner of the
Hubbub coucht,
Make Game of that which
makes as much of Thee.

XLVI

For in and out, above, about,
below,
'Tis nothing but a Magic
Shadow-show
Play'd in a Box whose Candle
is the Sun,
Round which we Phantom
Figures come and go.

XLVII

And if the Wine you drink,
the Lip you press,
End in the Nothing all
Things end in—Yes—
Then fancy while Thou art,
Thou art but what
Thou shalt be—Nothing—
Thou shalt not be less.

XLVIII

While the Rose blows along
the River Brink,
With old Khayyám the Ruby
Vintage drink:
And when the Angel with his
darker Draught
Draws up to Thee—take that,
and do not shrink.

XLIX

'Tis all a Chequer-board of
Nights and Days
Where Destiny with Men for
Pieces plays:
Hither and thither moves,
and mates, and slays,
And one by one back in the
Closet lays.

L

The Ball no Question makes of
Ayes and Noes,
But Right or Left as strikes
the Player goes;
And He that toss'd Thee
down into the Field,
He knows about it all—He
knows—He knows!

LI

The Moving Finger writes;
and, having writ,
Moves on: nor all thy Piety
nor Wit
Shall lure it back to cancel
half a Line,
Nor all thy Tears wash out a
Word of it.

LII

And that inverted Bowl we
call The Sky,
whereunder crawling coop't
we live and die,
Lift not thy hands to It for
help—for It
Rolls impotently on as Thou
or I.

LIII

With Earth's first Clay They
did the Last Man's Knead,
And then of the Last Harvest
sow'd the Seed:
Yea, the first Morning of
Creation wrote
What the Last Dawn of
Reckoning shall read.

LIV

I tell Thee this—when,
starting from the Goal,
Over the shoulders of the
flaming Foal
Of Heav'n and Parwin and
Mushtara they flung,
In my predestined Plot of
Dust and Soul.

LV

The Vine had struck a Fibre;
which about
If clings my Being—let the
Sufi flout;
Of my Base Metal may be
filed a Key,
That shall unlock the Door he
howls without.

LVI

And this I know: whether the
one True Light,
Kindle to Love, or Wrath
consume me quite,
One glimpse of It within the
Tavern caught
Better than in the Temple lost
outright.

LVII

Oh, Thou, who didst with
Pitfall and with Gin
beset the Road I was to
wander in,
Thou wilt not with
Predestination round
Enmesh me, and impute my
Fall to Sin?

LVIII

Oh, Thou, who Man of baser
Earth didst make,
And who with Eden didst
devise the Snake;
For all the Sin wherewith the
Face of Man
Is blacken'd, Man's
Forgiveness give—and take!

Kaza-Nama

LIX

Listen again. One evening at
the Close
Of Ramazán, ere the better
Moon arose,
In that old Potter's Shop I
stood alone
With the clay Population
round in Rows.

LX

And, strange to tell, among
the Earthen Lot
Some could articulate, while
others not:
And suddenly one more
impatient cried—
'Who is the Potter, pray, and
who the Pot?'

LXI

Then said another—'Surely
not in vain
My substance from the
common Earth was ta'en,
That He who subtly wrought
me into Shape
Should stamp me back to
common Earth again.'

LXII

Another said—'Why, ne'er a
peevish Boy,
would break the Bowl from
which he drank in Joy;
Shall He that made the Vessel
in pure Love
And Fancy, in an after Rage
destroy!'

LXIII

None answer'd this; but after
Silence spake
A Vessel of a more ungainly
Make:
'They sneer at me for leaning
all awry;
what! did the Hand then of
the Potter shake?'

LXIV

Said one—'Folks of a surly
Tapster tell,
And daub his Visage with the
Smoke of Hell;
They talk of some strict
Testing of us—Pish!
He's a Good Fellow, and 'twill
all be well.'

LXV

Then said another with a
long-drawn Sigh,
'My Clay with long oblivion
is gone dry:
But, fill me with the old
familiar Juice,
Methinks I might recover
by-and-by!'

LXVI

So while the Vessels one by
one were speaking,
One spied the little Crescent
all were seeking:
And then they jogg'd each
other, 'Brother, Brother!
Hark to the Porter's
Shoulder-knot a creaking!'

LXVII

Ah, with the Grape my fading
Life provide,
And wash my Body whence
the Life has died,
And in a Windingsheet of
vine-leaf wrapt,
So bury me by some sweet
Garden-side.

LXVIII

That ev'n my buried Ashes
such a Snare
Of Perfume shall fling up
into the Air,
As not a True Believer
passing by
But shall be overtaken
unaware.

LXIX

Indeed the Idols I have loved
so long
Have done my Credit in
Men's Eye much wrong:
Have drown'd my Honour in
a shallow Cup,
And sold my Reputation for a
Song.

LXX

Indeed, indeed, Repentance
oft before
I swore—but was I sober
when I swore?
And then and then came
Spring, and Rose-in-hand
My thread-bare Penitence
apieces tore.

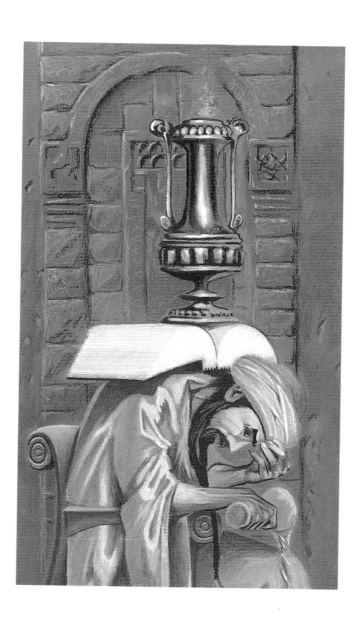

LXXI
And much as Wine has
play'd the Infidel,
And robb'd me of my Robe of
Honour—well,
I often wonder what the
vintners buy
One half so precious as the
Goods they sell.

LXXII
Alas, that Spring should
vanish with the Rose!
That Youth's sweet-scented
Manuscript should close!
The Nightingale that in the
Branches sang,
Ah, whence, and whither
flown again, who knows!

LXXIII
Ah, Love! could thou and I
with Fate conspire
To grasp this sorry Scheme of
Things entire,
Would not we shatter it to
bits—and then
Re-mould it nearer to the
Heart's Desire!

LXXIV
Ah, Moon of my Delight, who
know'st no wane,
The Moon of Heav'n is rising
once again:
How oft hereafter rising shall
she look
Through this same Garden
after me—in vain!

LXXV

And when Thyself with
shining Foot shall pass
Among the Guests Star-
scatter'd on the Grass,
And in thy joyous Errand
reach the Spot
Where I made one—turn
down an empty Glass!

Tamám Shud